Loving Levi ~ A millennial mother's guide for becoming a "bonus mom"

By

Stacey Nchanji

Dedication

For my mother,

Thank you for empowering me to be the mother I am today.

I love you always

~Stacey

Preface

"I love you, Mommy!" Aren't those the sweetest words anybody can ever hear? I am blessed to have the sweetest, most kind-hearted bonus child on the planet! Of course, everybody believes this to be true about their own children, but it's not as common when it comes to bonus children. I'm a 40-year-old married mother of three. Two of my children are biological, and the third, I call my bonus child. I do not even like the term stepchild. It simply does not exist in my vocabulary. Levi is my child! It is true I did not give birth to him, nor did I have the pleasure of carrying him in my belly, but he is my child. I don't believe I could love him any more if I had.

In this day and age, many of us start our parenting journey as stepparents (ewww, that word—it puts a bad taste in my mouth to even type it). However, it is the politically correct term. Throughout this book, however, I will use the term bonus child, because I believe that to be true. The Cambridge Dictionary defines a bonus as: a pleasant extra thing. Therefore, anything anybody receives as a bonus is always positive, and so is my beloved Levi.

The purpose of this book is to guide those in a situation like mine. My story is unique, and I will address that throughout the text. However, I hope that it will be a good resource for those in similar situations. Let it be clear: I have no psychology degree, and I am no relationship expert—I'm simply a millennial mother who was also blessed enough to be a bonus mom. Let's get into it!

Table of Contents

Introduction

The book will be broken into 7 sections, each of which will go over topics that I think are useful in navigating this journey. My second disclaimer is that this is an extremely emotionally taxing experience. You must have thick skin. Being a parent is hard enough as it is, as we all very well know. Nevertheless, I will make references for those who do not have any of their own children. However, most of my experience stems from having to deal with my own biological children as well as my bonus child. It will be a long, hard, often emotionally taxing journey, but I believe you can do it. Purchasing this book shows that you are committed to being the best bonus parent you can be. This is absolutely a great first step. I want to give you some encouragement: the journey is absolutely worth it, and the rewards are priceless!

To give a little background on my personal experience, as I mentioned before, I'm 40 years old. I became a bonus mom about seven years ago. Unfortunately, Levi's mom and I do not communicate at all. It is a cause of sadness for all of us, and I really hope it will change in the future. To be clear, I hold no ill will or negative feelings towards her. She, unfortunately, does not feel the same, and we're just going to leave it at that.

My apologies to the bonus dads. I wish I could speak intelligently about being a bonus dad, but seeing as though I am merely a mom, this is what I can speak about based on my experience. There are definitely some books that specifically discuss becoming a bonus dad. If you read my book, you may still get valuable input on preparing to be a bonus parent, regardless of whether you are a mom or a dad.

Chapter 1: Preparing yourself (put your feelings aside)

So, you've decided to become a bonus mom. Are you emotionally ready for such a great task? Raising any child is challenging, period! However, raising someone else's child compounds that difficulty. How will you react when they misbehave? Will you, in your heart of hearts, treat the child the same as you do your biological children? Will you be overcompensating by being too lenient? Will you possibly be a little sterner with them, as you may feel a certain amount of resentment towards them? These questions are all real and valid, so how do you prepare yourself for it?

When my son first came to stay with us, it was supposed to only be for the holidays. We were to have him over New Year's, and he was to be returned to his grandfather's house, where he and his mother were residing at the time. However, a few days before we were supposed to drop him off, his grandfather informed us that his mother was unavailable to care for the child. Therefore, we could either take him (they would send him) in or send him to Africa.

At the time, we only had my older daughter, Edyn, my youngest, Ndinashe, had not been born yet. Ironically enough, Edyn was in Africa at the time, in an attempt to wean her off from breastfeeding. Needless to say, this meant that, for the introduction into the household, he was the only child, at least for a couple of weeks. Under these circumstances, I really didn't have a chance to prepare myself mentally for having him stay with us permanently. I was prepared for a week's visit, and he would return to his mother's care.

We had a court-ordered visit arrangement that stated we would get him one weekend a month, every other major holiday, and Father's Day. Until now, we have only managed to have one visit with him. He met his sister then, and we took them to Chuck E. Cheese. I will not go into too much detail as to why we were not allowed to see him, as the purpose of this book is not to bash his biological mother.

Okay, back to our conversation on mentally preparing yourself. Hopefully, your journey is not like mine, and you and the biological parents can actually hold a conversation before the child first visits. You can then at least know the child's needs and preferences beforehand. Simple things, like having their preferred cereal and snacks stocked, knowledge of any allergies, can really smooth this transition for both you and your bonus child.

The first thing to remember is that you are not trying to replace or compete with the biological parent. Your role is to be another trusted adult who cares for them—period. Simple as that... or is it?

The mental preparation can be quite taxing. You have married this person who you knew had a child from a previous relationship. Essentially, by default, you have accepted their children as yours. If you cannot or will not do this, you have no business attempting to be a bonus mom.

In a perfect world, your future spouse would let you know they have children. In an even more perfect world, you could meet them before you got married. Whether you've met them before the marriage or not, having them live with you is a whole other ball game. Let's go over both scenarios.

Scenario #1: You had the privilege of meeting your bonus baby before the marriage.

Regardless of their age, you would have had some level of interaction with them, perhaps during their visitation with your spouse. If this is the case for you, this is wonderful! You do not have to start from scratch. You have been able to interact with them, and you know their likes and dislikes, hobbies, etc. Preparations are ten times easier, as you are continuing a relationship not creating one.

Scenario #2: You did not meet your bonus child prior to the marriage.

This is the main premise of this book: a scenario in which you haven't had interactions with the child, or they've been limited. Either you will meet for the first time, they will be around you overnight, for an extended period, or they will move in with you permanently. In either scenario, there is a mental battle you have to win.

As a bonus mom, you are in quite a predicament if the biological parent and your spouse were previously married. There will be high emotions from the child, regardless of their age. The mental battle I mentioned above is whether you can navigate through those angry, resentful, negative feelings. Can you be an adult, set your feelings aside, and realize that the child is going through something traumatic?

Whether the dissolution of their parents' relationship was amicable or not, picture yourself as a child. Your parents were together (hopefully, at some point, they were), and you were one big happy family, as far as you knew. Now, think back to the time when they separated and how that made you feel. Taking it further, now remember if/when a new person came around as a stepfather or stepmother. How did you feel toward that person, no matter how wonderful they were to you?

I'd like to be bold enough to say: most of us will know what that feels like in this generation. Therefore, I have

sympathy for the kid. They now have to be around this person, and whether or not they are the cause of their parents' separation, you would feel some feelings toward them. Once again, as the adult in the situation, you have to remember not to take this personally. Even though those feelings will be directed toward you, the child is processing a lot. Most adults do not know how to process big feelings. Therefore, a young child dealing with so much deserves additional grace. So, how does one prepare mentally?

Rule #1: Do not try to be their friend.

I repeat: do not try to be their friend—this is a recipe for disaster! Do be friendly. Depending on their age, tap into their hobbies and interests, and try to connect with them through those. Show them that you are also a bonus—and who doesn't love bonuses? You are to be an extra adult who loves, cares for, and nurtures them.

Depending on some dynamics, it may be hard for you at first. You must establish trust and build bonds with them, which inevitably takes time. I was lucky enough not to really struggle with bonding and trust. Levi was a little over two when he started living with us. I was a little nervous and worried about him not warming up to me. I assumed that by two, he should have had a strong bond with his mother and some amount of stranger danger. Surprisingly, I had quite the opposite experience. It actually worried me that he had absolutely no form of stranger danger at ALL!

My sweet boy—so loving, so affectionate, so emotionally intelligent. However, his affinity for complete strangers was utterly alarming to me. Naturally, he had a great bond with his father, and as a bonus mom, I made it my foremost goal to create my own bond with him.

Rule #2: Give yourself and the child time to form a bond

As mentioned in Rule #1, forming a bond takes time. There is no magical wand that you can wave to magically create this wonderful connection with a child you have just met. It does not work with adults, and it will not work with a child. Be kind to yourself and to the child. You are more than likely fumbling through it awkwardly. You do not really know how to relate to them, and that is okay, as long as you are putting forth effort.

Kids are very intelligent, and they will recognize that you are trying. Whether they receive it or not is another question. Regardless of whether they're receptive is up to them. If you have made an attempt, they will recognize that.

Rule #3: Be prepared for rejection

Sad as it is, no matter how hard you try, no matter how well you prepare, the child may still completely reject you. This is an unlikely, but very real, possibility. Most children, regardless of their age, are reasonable enough to see when a person means them no harm. It may take a while, depending on their outlook, but if you are consistent in your consideration, patience, and love toward them, they will inevitably come around.

In the unlikely event that they do reject you, you will have to prepare yourself for how you will navigate your relationship with them. Refer to Rule #1: You still do not want to try and be their friend. You are an adult, and they are a child. I advise that you be friendly, and if they are not receptive, then you need to be at least cordial. Continue to let them feel included and loved, whether they reciprocate it or not.

As the adult, you must mentally develop thick skin as an additional nurturer. Naturally, as I previously mentioned, there may be some tinges of resentment. The resentment typically is not toward you personally, but toward the situation they now find themselves in. The resentment might manifest itself in hurtful words, manipulation, and outright insubordination. You might even hear the dreaded, "You're not my mom!" yelled at you. Pure venom to a bonus parent's heart, right? You're doing your best to integrate, accept, and bond with this child, and that will be the thanks you get. Set your feelings aside.

The child is actually right. You are not their mother. You are a mother figure. You will need to have this conversation with your bonus child, with your spouse present. Explain that you are not trying to replace their mother. The child is probably hurt, confused, and disappointed that their parents' relationship is over. Give them grace and be patient. Set your feelings aside.

As previously mentioned, you, the bonus mom, may be a product of a blended family, so you know firsthand what it feels like. Recall the first time you met and had to interact with your stepmother or father. Recall the whirlwind of emotions you felt, including the guilt you felt if you actually liked them. You felt like you were somehow betraying your mother. The feeling that you cannot be neutral. You are caught in the middle, and in actuality, did not know how to feel.

Enter rule #4 Prepare for the impact it will have on you and your spouse's relationship

Whether or not you and your bonus child are getting along, forming a bond, and getting used to each other will influence your relationship with your spouse. It may be positive, or it may be negative. They may appreciate the way that you're treating their child and fall even deeper in love with you. On the flip side, they may see your lack of connection and wonder why you cannot get along with their child.

The relationship may become strained due to their child acting out. Your inability to deal with an irrational child could cause a rift between the two of you. In contrast, they may distance themselves or get frustrated with their child for not behaving well, not accepting you, or not treating you as a parent figure. They may overcompensate by being too lenient or becoming too strict with their child.

Your role as a bonus mom is to balance that disconnect. All children should be treated the same within the household—biological or otherwise—and there should be no special treatment based on their biological makeup. You and your spouse need to be on the same page about this, or it may open the door to manipulation and insubordination.

Rule #5: Recognize that being a parent is hard

At any age, at any stage in life, your children are a source of your greatest joy and your greatest stress. Whatever they do, you love them through it. They may disappoint you, they may hurt you, but you love them, nonetheless. This concept may be hard to reconcile because you did not carry this child or bring them into the world.

To make it relatable, think about the people who adopt children. Imagine the type of love that they have for those children. They not only desired a child but also underwent rigorous screening to acquire the honor of being that child's parent. You, my friend, get the exact privilege for free! That is the type of love you should have for your bonus child: profound and unconditional.

Just like your biological children, they should never feel that there's anything they could do that would cause you to stop loving them. This is the ultimate test of being a bonus parent. It is absolutely not easy—it is absolutely the hardest, most grueling part of it. However, if you accept that this is your child and eliminate the mindset of "stepmom," as I have, you are on the path to success!

You will need to have an open and honest conversation with your spouse. You will be undertaking a lot. It will be emotionally taxing at times, it will get hard, and things may get heated. Hopefully, you will form a united front. You and your spouse have to adopt the same parenting style. I tend to be more of the disciplinarian, and my husband is more lenient, but the rules are the rules.

The children know they cannot play us against each other. They know that if one of us says no, then that is "our" answer. Even in the few instances where I would allow them to do something, and my husband has said no, then that is still "our" answer. I may share that I would have permitted it away from them and outside their earshot, but never in their presence. Remember, you MUST be a united front.

Parenting style alignment is essential! There are no favorites. The consequences for a particular wrongdoing are the same across the board. All discipline is age-appropriate and non-gender-specific. We do not apply discipline to Levi that we would not with our daughters.

Rule #6: Consider therapy

I am a strong advocate for therapy, and before and after you have this interaction, a priceless resource would be to seek some sort of counseling for all the parties involved. That being said, all the counseling in the world is not going to help the child adjust if they don't feel safe around you. If they don't feel like your intentions are pure and you wish the world for them. If they feel even the slightest tinge of favoritism towards your biological children, imagine how that might make them feel. Imagine how out of place you would feel. Now, imagine being a toddler, a young child, or a teenager, dealing with all these emotions. The expectation is that they should be a loving angel and regulate those emotions, right? Most adults don't even know how to regulate their emotions, and yet we expect a confused child to.

You just have to give your bonus children some grace. They are dealing with a lot of big emotions. You have to be extra careful about the way you treat them. I'm not asking you to be overly lenient. I'm not asking you to bend the rules for them either— just be really matter of fact and deliberate with the way that you interact with this child. Sufficiently prepare yourself and everyone else in the household for the transition.

Have a family meeting with your biological children and spouse before they arrive. The day they arrive, have another meeting, a sort of pep talk on how great it is going to be to have a bonus brother or sister, and how excited you are to have a bonus baby! Time to put your big-girl panties on, saddle up, and go on this wild but rewarding ride!

So, you have decided to bring this child into our household. You have had a conversation with our partner about what the rules are, and the parenting style is aligned. One of the most stressful situations that could arise with bonus children is one where they try to manipulate the two of you. In your quest to build a bond with this child, you must remember that you are still a parent figure. I will repeat this again: you cannot be their friend. I hold that true for my biological children, the same as my bonus baby. I have no desire to be their friend. I want them to love and respect me. I would like them to like me, but I know there are times when they will not. I know this will also hold true for Levi. There will be times when he may dislike me, but he will always respect and love me. I want my children to know they can come and tell me when they've made a mistake. I want them to know that it is okay to make mistakes, but they must also learn that there are consequences for their actions. As with discipline, consequences are universal in our household.

So, you have discussed discipline, you've prepared your home for your bonus child, but what is the final step? This is actually the first step, but I saved it for last so that it will resonate the most with this chapter. Lean in for this one... are you ready? Okay, here it is... **set your feelings aside**! Whatever your interaction with the biological parent, it is ALL about your bonus child. If you are incapable of doing this, then do not be with or marry someone who already has children. You are unqualified for the job and will inevitably fail at it. All that matters is their well-being, their adjustment, and their comfort.

Chapter 2: Preparing your home

You have prepared yourself mentally, emotionally, and maybe even physically for your bonus baby. Part of this process is preparing your home for their arrival. You need to create a space for them. Create an age- and gender-appropriate space for them, as far as their living and sleeping arrangements are concerned. When he joined us, Levi shared a room with his sister, Edyn. They had two toddler beds next to each other. It was an appropriate setting because he was two and she was one. If you have an older bonus child, obviously, gender comes into play. Therefore, do your best to prepare an area that will allow them to have a space that's their own in your house, even if it's not an entire room.

Empty a chest drawer or a shelf, and provide toiletries, etc. Do your best to make them feel welcome and at home. I would also suggest you get to know their likes and dislikes. Levi was two, so he liked building blocks, cars, and dinosaurs—not hard to figure out.

If they are a bit older, and you don't have a rapport with their mom, ask their dad, or even better, ask them directly. It will go a long way if you make an effort to make them feel comfortable in your home. You may even want to buy them a welcome gift. You have to be strategic about this, though. You do not want it to be viewed as you trying to buy their affection, but rather that you are just so excited to meet and have them be a part of your blended family.

If they will only be visiting you, purchase a few sets of pajamas, underwear, and other overnight supplies. This, once again, reinforces your desire to have them feel at home. It also eliminates the need for them to haul those things between you and their biological parent all the time. If they are staying with you permanently, hopefully, they will bring all their clothes with them, but it would still be a nice gesture if you bought a couple of new items for the transition.

You may even use clothes shopping as an opportunity to bond with your bonus child by allowing them to be part of the process. Children like to be heard and seen, unlike previous generations, when we were asked to do the opposite. Your bonus child will appreciate that you want them to feel seen and valued and also that you care about their preferences. As mentioned above, this is an excellent time to form a bond and have a one-on-one outing.

One-on-one interactions have a multitude of benefits. The lack of interruption from other people and audiences allows the child to be their authentic self with you. They do not feel like they are on display and have to react in a certain way based on who is around them. Also, who doesn't love shopping?

So, your bonus baby has arrived. Everybody is excited and welcoming. I suggest making his/her favorite meal if you know it. Hopefully, we're given the opportunity to welcome them with a hug if they're comfortable. It's okay if you aren't, but a huge smile and display of excitement is a must. You should have previously discussed with your spouse what your baby bonus will call you—by your first name, Ms. Stacey, or mom. Whatever you decide, it is good to have it decided beforehand. Your spouse can then introduce you by the decided term, and it can avoid or reduce the awkwardness.

Personally, my African upbringing could not bring me to allow a two-year-old to call me by my first name. I would have accepted Ms. Stacey, but my husband preferred that he call me mommy, and he just naturally did. It is all a matter of preference and what you and your spouse are comfortable with. I would also like to point out that while you and your spouse might be comfortable with a certain term, your bonus baby may not be. Don't force the issue. I'd say let it go until you form a bond, and then possibly slide it into a casual conversation: "I would really like it if you would call me…." Once again, don't stress or push the issue. Set your feelings aside!

Levi has always called me mommy; that's all he knows. He knows he has two mothers. The way we explained it to him is: "You have two aunties, Aunty Rumbi and Aunty Charlene, you have two uncles, Uncle Leslie and Uncle Tre, you have two grandpas, etc., well, you are super lucky and have two mommies—one that carried you in her belly and the one that you live with." He was six years old at the time we explained this to him, so that was an age-appropriate way to break it down for him.

Okay, so you've decided what your bonus child will call you. Great! Welcome hug, time to sit down and have a welcome/family meeting. Your spouse should facilitate this meeting and take the lead for the best delivery. You don't want your baby to feel like they have entered a military camp with a new drill sergeant barking out orders. Have your spouse introduce everyone individually. Have your spouse lay out house rules. Yes, there must be rules from day one. You cannot gradually ease into this, as it will create an opportunity for conflict in the future.

It must be established that the rules exist and there are consequences for not following them. It must also be clear that the rules of your household may not be identical to those of their biological parents, but they are still expected to follow them. Some of the rules that you should establish, regardless of their age, are: bedtime, age-appropriate chores, curfew, acceptable as well as unacceptable behavior, and finally, the consequences for breaking the rules. It is unfair for them not to know what is expected of them. You, too, should share what they can expect from you and allow them to ask questions and voice concerns.

Once everyone is up to speed on how the household will be run, show them around a bit. Give a grand tour of their new dwelling. Show them where they can put their things, where they will sleep, what bathroom to use, where to get extra supplies, the kitchen, etc. As part of the tour, include any items or rooms that are off-limits to them. Always best to set boundaries right off the jump. For example, perhaps your bonus baby is used to watching TV while they eat.

We all sit at the table and eat most of the meals together at our house. So, reinforce that rules may differ at your house. Make statements such as, "We are just so excited to have you here, we want to get to know you, and what better way than to do so over dinner? We use meals as times to check in, see how everyone's day went, and catch up on any fun and exciting things. I know it is different from what you are used to, but I know you will learn to love it and even look forward to it!" This acknowledges their feelings while establishing the rule and hopefully avoiding resistance.

Another point of interest would be establishing chores. You could approach it by saying, "Hey Levi, after dinner we typically scrape our plates and put them in the sink. We take turns loading the dishwasher, and today is Edyn's turn. Tomorrow is Ndina's, and the next day we'd like you to take your turn." Most kids are eager to help and seek approval from adults. They will really surprise you with their desire to jump right into the household routine.

During the week, our schedules are super hectic with school, work, and extracurriculars. In our home, Saturday mornings are when everyone gets weekend chores. Everybody wipes down their bathroom counter and vacuums their room. I don't expect my kids to make their bed every day because I myself do not, but if you do, power to ya. Anyways, Saturdays: everybody also changes their linen and makes their bed. My kids, aged 9, 8 and 5, help with their laundry by bringing their hampers down, loading the washer, starting it, loading the dryer when ready, and putting them back into their hamper. I help them sort and fold it, and then they return it to their closet and chest of drawers. Structure and the development of life skills are key.

As I previously mentioned, you need to hold a family meeting before the baby bonus arrives. The attendees of this meeting are your biological children and your spouse. You should explain what is about to happen to your children, allow them to share how they feel, and prepare them for what's ahead.

If they have any reservations or anxiety, try to ease them before your bonus baby arrives. Assure them that your love and affection for them will remain the same. Assure they will just gain a new brother/sister and consider them a bonus. We all love bonuses! Siblings will squabble, that's expected; however, what we are trying to avoid is the dreaded, "That's my mommy!" being uttered by your biological children. If your child ever says it, be sure and correct them immediately. "Edyn, we don't intentionally say things to hurt other people's feelings." Make them understand that they are all your children and you love them the same.

You should leave the welcome/family meeting feeling light, not too stern or militant, just set expectations and let everybody acclimate to the new environment. I suggest you then go about your normal routine. Do not be too ceremonious and make too much of a big deal. Extravagance, such as a "welcome to the family party," might intimidate, frustrate, and confuse the child. It is a lot to take in all at once.

They may shy away, go to their room, and isolate themselves. Your job is to try to include them as much as possible. Do not be pushy. Do not be militant. Please do not force them to participate in anything they don't want to. Instead, give warm suggestions. For example, you could ask them if they'd like to join a board game or something else you can all participate in. Perhaps pick a movie, pop some popcorn, and watch it as a family. Something that can engage them without being too heavy and requiring too much from them. Remember, they are also processing their feelings and trying to make sense of it all. So, give them grace and set your feelings aside!

Chapter 3: Welcoming your bonus baby

Preparing the Physical Space: More Than Just a Room

When your partner's child (or children) steps across the threshold of your shared home for the first time (or for an extended period), a new chapter in your life begins. It's a moment filled with anticipation, perhaps a touch of anxiety, and the immense potential for building lasting connections. This chapter focuses on creating a welcoming and comfortable environment, laying the groundwork for a positive stepparent-stepchild (I just hate this term) relationship.

Creating a welcoming environment goes beyond simply setting up a bedroom. It's about fostering a sense of belonging and making your bonus baby feel like they have a space that's truly theirs. Personalization is key. If possible, involve your bonus baby in decorating their room. Let them choose colors, bedding, and personal items. This allows them to express their individuality and create a space that reflects their personality. Here is a list of other key areas to be aware of:

Familiar Comforts: Include familiar items from their biological parents' home, such as favorite toys, books, or photos. This can help ease the transition and provide a sense of continuity. Also, ensure space for your bonus baby in common areas. Create a designated spot for their belongings in the living room or kitchen. Display family photos that include them, reinforcing their place in the family.

Respecting Privacy: Your bonus baby may need time and space to adjust. Please respect their privacy and avoid intruding on their personal space.

Safety First: Ensure your home is safe and child-proof. Address any potential hazards and create a secure environment.

Preparing the Emotional Space: Building Bridges of Trust: Creating a welcoming emotional environment is just as important as preparing the physical space. It's about building trust, fostering open communication, and demonstrating genuine care.

Open and Honest Communication: Initiate conversations with your bonus child about their feelings and expectations. Listen actively and validate their emotions, even if you don't fully understand them.

Patience and Understanding: Remember that building a relationship takes time. Be patient and understanding, especially during the initial adjustment period. Avoid rushing the process and allow your bonus baby to set the pace.

Respecting Boundaries: Be mindful of your bonus child's boundaries. Avoid asking intrusive questions or pushing for intimacy before they're ready.

Creating Shared Experiences: Plan activities you and all your children can enjoy together. This could involve playing games, watching movies, walking, or exploring new hobbies. Shared experiences create opportunities for bonding and building positive memories.

One-on-One Time: If there are multiple bonus children, dedicate one-on-one time to each. This shows them that you value their individual relationships and are invested in getting to know them.

Positive Reinforcement: Offer positive reinforcement for their efforts and accomplishments. Celebrate their successes and encourage their passions. Use statements like, "I'm so proud of you!" "I knew you could do it!" and "Great job, buddy!"

Navigating Existing Dynamics: Be aware of the existing dynamics between your partner and their child(ren). Avoid interfering with or trying to change their established relationship. Instead, focus on building your own unique connection.

Managing Expectations: Avoid setting unrealistic expectations for yourself or your bonus baby. Building a strong relationship takes time, effort, and mutual respect.

Co-parenting Considerations: If applicable, respect the co-parenting relationship and avoid speaking negatively about the other parent. Support your partner in maintaining healthy communication with their ex.

The First Few Days: Setting the Tone

The first few days are crucial for setting the tone for your stepparent-stepchild relationship. Keep it low-key. Avoid overwhelming your bonus baby with too many activities or social interactions. Allow them time to settle in and adjust to their new surroundings.

Establish routines. Consistent routines can provide a sense of stability and predictability, which is especially important for children who are experiencing significant changes. Shared meals are a great time and tool for bonding and conversation. Create a relaxed and welcoming atmosphere at the dinner table.

As a bonus mom, your role is to listen more than you speak. Pay attention to your bonus child's cues and listen more than you speak. This shows them that you're genuinely interested in getting to know them. Remember, however, to be yourself. Authenticity is key to building trust. Be yourself and let your bonus baby get to know the real you.

Welcoming your bonus child(ren) into your home is a significant milestone. Creating a welcoming environment, building bridges of trust, and setting a positive tone can lay the foundation for a strong and loving bonus parent-bonus child relationship. Remember that patience, understanding, and genuine care are essential ingredients for success.

Chapter 4: Respecting the biological parent (knowing your place)

So, we've made it through the first meeting or visit. Everyone's settling in and following the rules. The siblings are playing well together, getting along, and we are a regular old Brady Bunch, right? Well, not typically. This takes a lot of time, patience, and positive reinforcement. Your relationship with the biological mother will be a key element to this progression and development. Unfortunately, most bonus moms are met with animosity from biological ones. The dreaded, "I don't want that woman around my kids!" "You better not leave my kids alone with her," etc.

In a perfect world, there would be no baby mama drama. She enjoys her time away from her kids and appreciates you're caring for them during that time. She realizes that it is essential for their child's wellbeing that they have a relationship with their father and therefore, does not use them as pawns to try and spite him. Perfect world scenario! Yeah, right! Okay, well, I'm going to discuss three scenarios: perfect world, no contact, and baby mama drama galore!

Perfect World

In a perfect world, your spouse had an amicable split from the other biological parent. There are no hard feelings; everyone simply wants the best for the child(ren). As the bonus parent, you have a civil relationship with the biological parent. You communicate well, share occasions such as graduations, sports games, recitals, and birthdays. Your spouse and the biological parent are on good terms, interact well, and the child witnesses a mutually respectful relationship.

As a bonus mom, you are involved in the child's life and collaborate with the biological parent in all co-parenting matters. You never feel disrespected. They know their place and do not try to weaponize their position. Visitation is on schedule unless otherwise discussed. There may not even be a formal custody order or child support in place because everyone gets along royally. Sounds too good to be true, doesn't it? Well, that's because it is not a typical occurrence.

No contact

Unfortunately, this is the category I fall into. The biological mom wants nothing to do with the bonus mom, for whatever reason. It is usually understandable if infidelity played a part in the separation of the parties. If they feel like you "stole" their spouse, then it is natural that they will not want to get all chummy with you.

In such a situation, you need to have real and tough conversations with your spouse, as they are the only line of communication to the other parent. Typically, you will hear condensed hearsay, which complicates things. The lack of communication allows children to manipulate their parents more easily. If they ask something of one parent and they say no, they can go to the other and try their luck. This goes back to the united front I mentioned earlier. In instances where the answer is yes, manipulation can also creep in. For example, if they need money for an item for school and they ask both parental units, if both households say yes and provide the funds, the child now has extra unearned funds at their disposal because their parents cannot get along. This is probably the worst of these scenarios.

Baby Mama/Daddy Drama Galore

A close second to the no contact is the baby mama/daddy drama. In this instance, at least there is a line of communication, even if it is toxic. There is no mutual respect. Parties discuss the other parent negatively in front of the children. Statements like, "You're just like your daddy!" when they misbehave, yelling, cursing, and heated discussions in front of the children. Withholding visitation or not utilizing it. Dodging child support payments. Poisoning the child against the other parent by discussing adult topics, such as any infidelity that may have occurred. Competing with the bonus parent. Physical and verbal altercations. Attempts to break up the new relationship through advances or ignoring boundaries. The list goes on and on.

There is absolutely never any case when any of this is necessary. Imagine how your children feel watching that, feeling like they are the cause of it. Parents, please set your feelings aside! There has to be mutual respect for each other amongst all parties. Your children are watching and absorbing it all. They deserve better. They deserve stability and healthy relationships with both their parents without feeling guilty about it.

One of the most important things to remember when you become a stepparent is that you are not the child's biological parent. This means that you need to be respectful of the child's relationship with their biological parent. This can be a challenge, especially if you are used to being the primary caregiver for children. However, it is important to remember that the child's relationship with their biological parent is special and should be respected.

Here are some tips for respecting the biological parent:

- Don't try to replace the biological parent.

- Don't criticize the biological parent.

- Don't overstep your boundaries.

- Be patient.

- Be supportive.

Don't try to replace the biological parent.

It is important to remember that you are not the child's biological parent. You can't replace the child's biological parent, and you shouldn't try to. The child's relationship with their biological parent is special and important, and you should respect that.

Don't criticize the biological parent.

It is important to avoid criticizing the child's biological parent, even if you disagree with their parenting choices. This can be **difficult**, especially if you are in a co-parenting situation. However, it is important to remember that the child loves their biological parent, and criticizing them will only make the child feel uncomfortable.

Don't overstep your boundaries.

It is important to be aware of your boundaries as a bonus parent. You are not the child's parent and shouldn't try to act like you are. This means that you should avoid making decisions about the child's life, such as what school they go to, what activities they participate in, religious beliefs and practices, politics, etc. (unless the biological parent has no contact with their child).

Be patient.

Building a relationship with a bonus child takes time. It is important to be patient and understanding. Don't expect to be accepted overnight. It may take some time for the child to warm up to you.

Be supportive.

It is important to be supportive of the child's relationship with their biological parent. This means that you should encourage the child to spend time with their biological parent and avoid talking negatively about them.

In addition to the tips above, it is also important to remember that every family is different. What works for one family may not work for another. It is important to be flexible and to find what works best for your family. It is also important to remember that being a bonus parent is always a rewarding experience. It can be a challenge, but it can also be very rewarding. If you are willing to put in the effort, you can build a strong and loving relationship with your stepchild.

Okay, let's delve deeper into the nuances of respecting the biological parent and "knowing your place" as a bonus mom. This isn't about diminishing your role but rather clarifying it for the entire family's well-being.

The Delicate Dance of Authority

One of the most challenging aspects of bonus parenting is navigating the line between being a supportive adult and overstepping your boundaries. This is especially true when it comes to discipline and decision-making. Discipline should be shared, not a sole responsibility, among all the parents: yourself, your spouse, and the other biological parent. Avoid taking on the primary role of disciplinarian unless explicitly agreed upon by both biological parents. Your role should be more of a supportive, consistent presence.

As I previously shared, Levi was only two when he began living with us. Therefore, I was lucky to be afforded the opportunity to set the tone when it came to discipline. Unless it is an immediate safety concern, I suggest that if you observe behavior that needs addressing, discuss it privately with your partner. Let them take the lead in addressing the issue, respectfully offering your observations and suggestions. Focus on establishing house rules and expectations together with your partner, ensuring consistency.

Decision-making concerning your bonus baby — all your children, actually — should be collaborative, not unilateral. Major decisions concerning the child's education, health, or extracurricular activities should ideally involve both biological parents. Your input is valuable, but respecting the biological parents' right to make these decisions is essential. In your day-to-day life, focus on supporting the decisions made by the biological parents. If you have concerns, express them privately and constructively.

Another important aspect of knowing your role is the importance of consistency. Even if you're not the primary disciplinarian, consistency is crucial. You and your partner have set rules; enforce them. Never undermine your spouse's authority by contradicting them in front of the child. Consistency between both households is ideal. If possible, communication between both households will benefit the child.

Being a bonus mom often involves navigating complex emotional landscapes. Here's how to approach some common challenges:

Dealing with Negative Comments:

If your bonus child makes negative comments about their other biological parent, resist the urge to join in or offer your own criticisms. Instead, validate their feelings ("It sounds like you're feeling frustrated") and encourage them to talk to their parent directly. Avoid taking sides in conflicts between the biological parents. Your role is to remain neutral and supportive of your partner.

Handling Jealousy and Insecurity:

Your bonus child(ren) may experience jealousy or insecurity about your relationship with their parent. Reassure them that your love for your partner doesn't diminish their parents' love for them. Focus on building your own unique relationship with your bonus child(ren), separate from their relationship with their biological parent.

Respecting the Other Parent's Time:

Be respectful of the other parent's time with their child(ren). Avoid scheduling activities that interfere with their visitation or parenting time. Flexibility is very important if/when plans change.

You are trying to build bridges, not walls. Respecting the biological parent isn't about creating distance but building bridges. As with any relationship, communication is key! Encourage open and respectful communication between your partner and their ex. This can help minimize conflict and create a more harmonious environment for the children.

If appropriate and with the agreement of the biological parents, respectful, limited communication can be very helpful. The focus of any and all communication should be the child's well-being. Remember that the child's well-being is the top priority.

Put their needs above your own feelings and avoid engaging in behaviors that could harm them. A child that sees the adults in their life working together will have a much easier time.

By understanding and respecting the biological parent's role, you can create a more stable and supportive environment for your bonus child(ren), foster healthy relationships, and promote their overall well-being.

Alright, let's explore some more nuanced aspects of respecting the biological parent and navigating your role as a bonus parent.

The Power of Language and Framing

The words you use can significantly impact the dynamic between you, your bonus child(ren), and their biological parent. Avoid "My" vs "Their" Parent. Instead of referring to your partner as "my mom/dad" in front of your bonus child(ren), use their name or "your mom/dad." This reinforces that your partner is their parent first and foremost. Similarly, avoid phrases that imply ownership or replacement, such as "I'm your new mom/dad."

Positive Framing of the Other Parent:

Even if you have personal disagreements with the other parent, strive to maintain a positive or neutral tone when speaking about them in front of your bonus child(ren). Acknowledge and respect the other parent's role in the child's life. For example, "Your mom will be so excited to hear about your soccer game!" Be mindful of using "our" when referring to family events or decisions. While you are part of the family, it's essential to acknowledge that the child also has another family. Consider phrasing like, "When you're with your mom/dad, you can decide..." or "In both of our homes, we try to..."

Gift-Giving Etiquette:

Coordinate gift-giving with your partner and, if appropriate, with the other parent. Avoid giving extravagant gifts that could create competition or resentment, especially if your financial situation's vary drastically. It is good to remember that gifts are not a way to buy affection.

The Importance of Boundaries with Extended Family

Your extended family's interactions with your bonus child(ren) can also impact the dynamic with the biological parent. Take the time to educate your family on past and present dynamics. Explain to your family members the importance of respecting the biological parent and avoiding negative comments. Encourage your family to build their own relationships with your bonus child(ren) without undermining the other parent. Address any and all inappropriate behavior head-on. If your family members engage in behaviors that are disrespectful to the biological parent, address the issue privately and firmly. Set clear boundaries and expectations for your family's interactions with your bonus child(ren).

Respecting the Other Extended Family

It is also important to remember that your stepchild has another set of grandparents, aunts, uncles, and cousins. Respecting those relationships is also very important. As we have now mentioned several times, building a positive stepparent-stepchild relationship takes time, patience, and consistency. Trust is the foundation of any healthy relationship. Be consistent in your actions, keep your promises, and show genuine care and concern for your stepchild(ren).

Avoid Taking Things Personally

Your stepchild(ren) may sometimes say or do hurtful things. Try not to take these actions personally. They may be expressing their own confusion, frustration, or loyalty to their other parent.

Celebrating Small Victories

Acknowledge and celebrate small victories in your relationship with your bonus child(ren). These positive moments can reinforce your bond and create lasting memories. By consistently demonstrating respect for the biological parent and prioritizing the child's well-being, you can create a harmonious and supportive environment for your blended family.

Chapter 5: Blending the family (special occasions)

I personally have yet to experience an occasion where Levi's biological mother and I have to share a special event, such as a sports game, birthday party, or school function. Navigating special occasions and traditions in blended families will inevitably come up sooner or later.

Holidays, birthdays, and other special occasions can be particularly challenging for blended families. You always want to respect existing traditions. Be sensitive to your bonus child(ren) 's traditions and routines with their other parent. Avoid trying to replace or override these traditions.

Be flexible and willing to compromise on scheduling and activities. Engage the entire family in creating new shared traditions. While respecting existing traditions, also look for opportunities to create new shared traditions with your bonus child(ren) and your partner. These new traditions can help build a sense of unity and create positive memories.

Special occasions, such as holidays and birthdays, should be a time of joy and celebration for blended families. However, they can also be a source of stress and anxiety. This is because blended families often have to navigate a complex web of traditions, expectations, and emotions.

Here are some tips for navigating special occasions as a bonus mom:

Communicate Early and Often

One of the most important things you can do to ensure a smooth and enjoyable experience is to communicate early and often with your co-parent. This will help you coordinate schedules, plan activities, and avoid any potential conflicts.

Be Flexible and Respectful of Traditions

It is important to respect the traditions that your stepchildren have with their other parent. This may mean that you have to celebrate some holidays or birthdays on different days or at different times.

Create New Traditions

Creating new traditions can help foster a sense of unity and belonging in your blended family. These traditions can range from cooking a special meal together to going on a family outing.

Manage Expectations

It is important to manage your expectations for special occasions. Things may not always go according to plan, and it is important to be flexible and adaptable.

Focus on the Positive

Remember to focus on the positive aspects of blending your family. Special occasions can be a time to create lasting memories and strengthen your relationships. It is essential to involve your bonus children in the planning process. This will help them feel like they are a part of the family. Be patient and understanding—it may take some time for your blended family to adjust to new traditions and routines.

As always, seek professional help if needed. If you are struggling to navigate special occasions in your blended family, you may want to seek professional support.

Holidays

Coordinate schedules with your co-parent to ensure that your children have the opportunity to spend time with both of their parents. Be respectful of religious and cultural traditions. Create new traditions that everyone can enjoy.

Birthdays

Plan a special birthday celebration for your bonus child(ren). Ideally, the families can come together for this one day a year for the sake of the child. Parental unity will be more beneficial than having to host two separate birthday parties every single year, with each parent trying to outdo the other. Consider giving them a meaningful gift. Help them feel loved and appreciated.

Weddings

If you are planning to get married, be sure to involve your bonus children in the planning process and in the wedding party. Consider having a special ceremony to acknowledge your blended family. Make sure everyone feels included and welcome. If the ex-partner happens to get remarried, encourage your bonus baby to participate in that ceremony as well. Be supportive and excited for them to have another new bonus parent.

Remember, blending families takes time and effort. But by following these tips, you can create a happy and healthy blended family. There is usually an unspoken emotional rollercoaster during special occasions. These moments are often loaded with emotional baggage for adults and children in blended families.

The child may be feeling both loss and grief over their family makeup. For children, holidays and birthdays can trigger feelings of loss and grief related to the original family structure. Be sensitive to these emotions and allow them space to express themselves. Acknowledge that it's okay for them to miss the way things used to be.

The child may also struggle with loyalty conflicts

Children may feel torn between celebrating with your family and their other biological parent. Reassure them that it's okay to love and enjoy time with both families. Avoid creating situations where they feel they have to choose sides.

They are most likely also experiencing anxiety and uncertainty. Changes in routines and schedules can be unsettling for children, especially during holidays. Provide clear information about plans and expectations. Maintain as much consistency as possible to create a sense of stability. As a bonus mom, you may feel pressure to create "perfect" holiday experiences. Manage your expectations and focus on creating meaningful moments. Remember, the goal is to build connections, not to achieve a Hallmark movie ideal.

Here are some practical strategies for smoother celebrations:

Detailed Scheduling and Communication

Unless otherwise court-ordered, create a detailed schedule for holidays and birthdays, including visitation arrangements and planned activities. Share this schedule with everyone involved. Ideally, you could all use a shared calendar or app to coordinate schedules and avoid miscommunication. Remember, communication with the other biological parent is key—even if it is uncomfortable.

Flexibility and Compromise

Be prepared to be flexible and compromise on plans. Things rarely go exactly as planned, especially in blended families. Prioritize the children's needs and well-being over rigid adherence to traditions. For example, if it is your weekend or holiday and the biological parent needs to switch, be willing to make adjustments without making a fuss.

Creating Inclusive Traditions

Involve everyone in creating new traditions that reflect the blended family's unique identity. Consider incorporating elements from both families' traditions to create a sense of inclusivity. Allow for the creation of individual traditions as well, respecting everyone's personal preferences.

Gift-Giving Considerations

Coordinate gift-giving with your partner and, if appropriate, with the other biological parent. Avoid giving extravagant gifts that could create competition or resentment. Focus on thoughtful and meaningful gifts that reflect the children's interests. Agree upon a price threshold that requires consultation with the other parent—for example, any gift over $200 must be discussed by both households. Any items with a heartbeat must also be discussed with both households before they are purchased.

Managing Extended Family

Communicate with your extended family about the blended family dynamics and expectations for special occasions. Encourage them to be inclusive and welcoming of your bonus child(ren). Address any inappropriate comments or behaviors from family members. Educate them on the gift price threshold and avoid "spoiling" the child with an abundance of gifts.

Creating "Down Time"

Special occasions can be overwhelming. Schedule some downtime for everyone to relax and recharge. Allow for quiet moments and individual activities to prevent sensory overload and emotional fatigue.

Documenting Memories

Take photos and videos to capture the special moments and create lasting memories for your blended family. As old-fashioned as it sounds, a fun suggestion would be to create a family scrapbook or photo album to preserve these memories.

Differing Religious or Cultural Beliefs

As joyous as special occasions can be, they are also potential inlets for conflict. A major area where this could arise is differing religious or cultural beliefs. Be respectful of each family's traditions and find ways to incorporate them into celebrations. Educate yourselves and your children about each other's beliefs to foster understanding and tolerance.

Visitation Disputes

If visitation disputes arise, prioritize the children's needs and seek mediation or legal counsel if necessary. Avoid involving the children in adult conflicts. If a dispute arises, let your partner take the lead. In this instance, you really need to stay in your lane.

Feelings of Exclusion

Be mindful of creating situations where anyone feels excluded or left out. Make a conscious effort to include everyone in activities and conversations. By approaching special occasions with empathy, flexibility, and a focus on creating meaningful connections, you can transform potential conflict points into opportunities for building stronger family bonds.

Let's dive into the finer points of navigating special occasions, focusing on the long-term impact and the development of resilience within the blended family.

You Can Build Resilience Through Rituals and Routines

Special occasions are prime opportunities to build resilience within your blended family. Rituals and routines, even small ones, can create a sense of stability and predictability, particularly during times of change.

Develop consistent rituals for holidays and birthdays, such as specific meals, activities, or traditions. These rituals can provide a sense of continuity and comfort for children. These routines must be predictable. Maintain as much of the children's normal routines as possible during special occasions. This can help to minimize anxiety and create a sense of normalcy.

While routines are important, be prepared to be flexible and adapt to changing circumstances. Teach your children that unexpected changes are a normal part of life.

The way you handle special occasions in the early years of your blended family can have a lasting impact on your children's emotional well-being. Focus on creating positive memories that your children will cherish for years to come. These memories can help to strengthen family bonds and create a sense of belonging.

As the Bonus Mum, You Should Master Your Own Coping Skills

Use special occasions as opportunities to teach your children coping skills for dealing with change and adversity as well. Help them develop resilience and emotional intelligence. Special occasions can be a time to strengthen relationships between stepparents and stepchildren.

Bonus parents often put the needs of others before their own, especially during special occasions. However, self-care is essential for maintaining emotional well-being. As a bonus parent, you have some rights too. Make sure that you incorporate and exercise your rights from the get-go. You absolutely must set boundaries. Set boundaries for yourself and avoid overcommitting. It's okay to say no to requests that will overwhelm you.

You must also prioritize rest. Make sure you get enough rest and relaxation during special occasions. This will help you to manage stress and maintain your energy levels. Seek support when you need it. Don't hesitate to reach out to your partner, friends, or family members. Being a bonus parent is challenging, and it's important to have a support system in place.

Reflect After Each Special Occasion

After each special occasion, take some time to reflect on what went well and what could be improved. This will allow you to adjust to future events. Ultimately, blending families during special occasions aims to create a legacy of love and acceptance.

Special Occasions Are a Perfect Opportunity to Demonstrate Your Unconditional Love

Show your bonus baby that you love and accept them for who they are. Let them know that they are a valued and important part of your family. Use special occasions as opportunities to build a strong foundation for your blended family. Create a sense of unity, belonging, and love.

Model healthy relationships for your children by demonstrating respect, empathy, and communication. Show that a family can be built on love even with different backgrounds and pasts. Focusing on these long-term considerations can create meaningful and memorable special occasions that strengthen your blended family and foster resilience in your children.

Chapter 6: Check yourself

Being a bonus parent is a journey of constant learning and adaptation. It demands empathy, patience, and a willingness to examine your own thoughts and behaviors. This chapter focuses on the crucial practice of self-reflection, empowering you to "check yourself" and navigate the complexities of blended family life with greater awareness and effectiveness.

Be aware of the mirror within so you can recognize your triggers and biases. We all carry baggage from our past experiences, and these can significantly impact our interactions as both parents and bonus parents. It is important to identify your triggers. Be cognizant of what situations or behaviors trigger negative emotions in you. Is it defiance, whining, or a perceived lack of respect?

Understanding your triggers allows you to anticipate and manage your reactions. Acknowledge your biases. Be honest about any biases you might hold, whether conscious or unconscious. Do you unconsciously compare your bonus children to your biological children? Recognizing these biases is the first step toward overcoming them. For example, my only bias was the difference in Levi's and my other children's gender. I had to decide when to separate bath time and have him in his own room. Like most toddlers, he would follow me to the bathroom, but I had to determine when that was no longer appropriate. To make it fair, I made it universal: everyone needs privacy in the restroom, so everyone should go alone.

Part of checking yourself is acknowledging your past experiences and their influence. Reflect on how your childhood experiences, past relationships, or family dynamics might influence your current interactions. Unresolved issues can cloud your judgment and create unnecessary conflict.

Emotional regulation is fundamental. Managing your reactions as a bonus parent can be emotionally challenging. Learning to regulate your reactions is crucial for maintaining a healthy family environment. Create a mental pause button. When you feel your emotions escalating, take a moment to pause. Step away from the situation if necessary. This pause allows you to regain control and respond thoughtfully, rather than react impulsively.

Practice mindfulness techniques, such as deep breathing or meditation, to calm your nervous system. These techniques can help you stay present and grounded in the moment. Other great tools are journaling and self-talk. Journaling can be a powerful tool for processing your emotions and gaining self-awareness. Practice positive self-talk to challenge negative thoughts and beliefs.

Effective communication is essential for building strong relationships. Self-reflection can help you communicate more effectively. Practice active listening by paying attention to your bonus children's verbal and nonverbal cues. Show genuine interest in their thoughts and feelings. Try to see things from your bonus children's perspective. What might they be feeling or experiencing?

Empathy can help you understand their behavior and respond with compassion—practice "I" statements. Use "I" statements to express your feelings and needs without blaming or accusing your bonus child. For example, "I feel frustrated when..." rather than "You always...". It's important to master evaluating your actions and seeking feedback. Self-reflection involves evaluating your actions and seeking feedback from others.

Regular check-ins are paramount. Schedule regular check-ins with yourself to reflect on your interactions with your bonus children throughout your transition. What went well? What could you have done differently? Always seek feedback from your partner. Engage in open and honest communication with your partner about your stepparenting. Ask for their feedback and be open to constructive criticism.

As always, consider professional guidance. Consider seeking guidance from a therapist, counselor, or stepparenting coach. A professional can provide valuable insights and support. The journey of being a bonus parent is an ongoing process of growth. Self-reflection is an ongoing process, not a one-time event. Remember to embrace imperfection. Acknowledge that you will make mistakes. Learn from them and move forward. Perfection is not the goal; progress is.

Celebrate your strengths. Recognize and celebrate your strengths as a bonus parent, acknowledging your efforts and progress. Commit yourself to continuous learning. Stay open to learning and growing as a bonus parent. Read books, attend workshops, and seek out resources to enhance your skills. By consistently "checking yourself," you can cultivate greater self-awareness, emotional regulation, and communication skills. This will strengthen your relationship with all your children and create a more harmonious and fulfilling blended family experience.

Let us explore the "Check Yourself" concept further, delving into deeper layers of self-awareness and practical applications. For instance, the subtleties of unconscious behavior. Our unconscious behaviors often speak louder than our conscious intentions.

Nonverbal communication can give more insight than verbal communication. Pay attention to your nonverbal cues: facial expressions, body language, and tone of voice. These can convey messages that contradict your words. Are you unconsciously displaying frustration, impatience, or disapproval?

Microaggressions are statements, actions, or incidents perceived as subtle or unintentional discrimination against another person. Be aware of microaggressions, as these subtle or unintentional acts of discrimination or bias can erode trust and create feelings of exclusion. Even well-intentioned comments can be hurtful if they perpetuate stereotypes or invalidate someone's experience.

Be sure to examine your "parental filter." Do you unconsciously apply different standards or expectations to your bonus children compared to your biological children? Strive for fairness and consistency in your interactions.

This is where emotional intelligence comes into play. Emotional intelligence (EQ) is crucial for navigating the complexities of blended family life. Develop a deeper understanding of your own emotions and how they impact your behavior. Recognize your strengths and weaknesses as a bonus parent. Practice self-regulation techniques to manage your emotions and respond constructively to challenging situations.

Avoid impulsive reactions and strive for thoughtful responses such as:

Empathy

Cultivate empathy by putting yourself in your bonus children's shoes and understanding their perspective. Validate their feelings, even if you don't agree with them.

Social Skills

Enhance your social skills by practicing effective communication, active listening, and conflict resolution. Build positive relationships with your bonus children and other family members.

Here are some practical tools for self-reflection:

The "Three Whys" Technique

When you experience a negative emotion or react impulsively, ask yourself "why" three times. This technique can help you uncover the root cause of your emotional response.

The "Movie Lens" Exercise

Imagine you are watching a movie of your interactions with your bonus children. How would you describe your behavior? What messages are you conveying?

The "Day in Review" Journal

At the end of each day, write a brief review of your interactions with your children. What went well? What could have been handled better? What can you do to improve the relationship?

Seeking Outside Perspectives

Talk with a trusted friend, family member, or therapist about your stepparenting experiences. Speak to other bonus parents; there is a whole community out there. An outside perspective can provide valuable insights and feedback.

There is real value in vulnerability. The most important aspect is being able to admit your mistakes. Be willing to admit your mistakes and apologize to your bonus children. This demonstrates humility and builds trust. Share your feelings appropriately. Share your feelings with your stepchildren in an age-appropriate way. This can help them understand your perspective and build empathy. Authenticity is key to building genuine connections. Be yourself and avoid trying to be someone you're not.

The "Check Yourself" practice is not about self-criticism but rather about self-improvement. It's about cultivating greater awareness, emotional intelligence, and empathy to create a more harmonious and loving blended family.

Let us explore the "Check Yourself" chapter further, focusing on the systemic aspects of blended family dynamics and how individual self-reflection can impact the entire family system. Blended families are complex systems where each members' actions and emotions impact the entire group.

Recognize the different roles that family members play and how these roles influence interactions. Are you falling into a specific role (e.g., the rescuer or the peacekeeper) that may hinder healthy dynamics? Observe communication patterns within the family. Are there recurring conflicts or misunderstandings? How are conflicts resolved (or not resolved)?

When one member of the family system changes their behavior, it can create a ripple effect throughout the entire system. By practicing self-regulation, you can break negative cycles of communication and behavior. For example, if you typically react defensively, consciously choosing to listen and respond calmly can shift the dynamic of a conflict.

Your self-reflection and growth can serve as a model for your stepchildren and partner. Children learn by observing the adults in their lives. By demonstrating vulnerability and self-awareness, you create a safe space for others to do the same, fostering deeper connection and intimacy within the family.

External systems have a strong impact on blended families. These systems include schools, extended families, and legal systems. Be aware of how schools may view and interact with blended families. Advocate for your bonus children's needs and ensure they receive the support they require.

Recognize how extended family members may influence the blended family system. Set boundaries and communicate expectations clearly. Understand how legal and custody arrangements can impact the family system. Seek legal counsel when necessary to protect your stepchildren's best interests.

Recognize the importance of ongoing evaluation. Self-reflection is not a one-time event; it's an ongoing process of evaluation and adjustment. Conduct regular family reviews. Consider holding regular family reviews to discuss how things are going and address any concerns. This can create a space for open communication and problem-solving.

As part of your self-checks, seek feedback from trusted friends, family members, or professionals who can provide an objective perspective. This can help you identify blind spots and areas for growth. Blended families are constantly evolving. Be prepared to adapt to changing circumstances and adjust your approach as needed. Children grow and change, and so do family dynamics.

The goal is to create a thriving family system. Self-reflection aims to create a thriving family system where everyone feels loved, supported, and valued. By working together and supporting each other, blended families can build resilience and overcome challenges.

Create a sense of belonging for all family members, regardless of their biological relationship. Celebrate each family member's unique qualities and contributions. Understanding the systemic aspects of blended family dynamics and practicing ongoing self-reflection can create a positive and supportive environment for your entire family to thrive.

Chapter 7: Enjoy the journey

While often challenging, stepparenting is also a journey filled with opportunities for growth, love, and connection. This chapter encourages you to embrace the adventure, find joy in the everyday moments, and celebrate the unique beauty of your blended family.

It is essential to shift your perspective. Shift your view of this dynamic from challenge to opportunity. It's easy to get caught up in the challenges of stepparenting, but shifting your perspective can transform your experience. Always focus on the positives. Actively look for the positive aspects of your blended family. Celebrate the small victories and acknowledge the progress you've made.

Remind yourself of the unique strengths and qualities of your bonus children. Be flexible and embrace the unexpected. Blended family life is rarely predictable. Embrace the unexpected twists and turns and learn to adapt to change. See challenges as opportunities for growth and learning. Practice gratitude by focusing on the things you appreciate in your life and family; this will cultivate a sense of gratitude. You might even keep a gratitude journal or share daily affirmations with your partner.

Parenting is a rewarding experience! Finding joy in everyday moments makes it all the more worthwhile. Joy isn't always found in grand gestures; it's often hidden in the simple moments of everyday life. The most basic daily task can be an opportunity to connect through shared activities. Engage in activities that you and your bonus children enjoy together, whether playing games, watching movies, or going for walks. These shared experiences create opportunities for bonding and connection.

It's all about celebrating the small victories. Acknowledge and celebrate even the smallest achievements of your bonus children. Positive reinforcement can build their confidence and strengthen your relationship. Finding humor in the chaos is an excellent technique. Blended family life can be chaotic at times. Find humor in the everyday mishaps and don't take yourself too seriously. Laughter can be a powerful tool for bonding and stress relief.

Create meaningful rituals as a family; Establish meaningful rituals that bring your family together, such as family dinners, bedtime stories, or weekend outings. Every Monday, we create a Soul Train-like tunnel—just the five of us. We high-five each other as we pass through and sing that " Aaron Pierre, that's Mufasa song. This is our beginning-of-the-week ritual to motivate everyone and encourage them to have a great school/work week.

Rituals such as these create a sense of belonging and connection. The goal is to build strong relationships; it is a journey of the heart. The core of stepparenting is building strong, loving relationships. Prioritize your connection with your bonus to children. Always make time for one-on-one interactions with all your children. Show genuine interest in their lives, interests, and feelings.

As the adult who chose this role, always practice empathy and understanding. Remember, the child did not choose to be your bonus child; however, you chose to be their bonus parent. Strive to understand your bonus children's perspective and empathize with their experiences. Validate their feelings, even if you don't fully understand them.

Communicate openly and honestly; children can smell a phony person a mile away. Encourage open and honest communication within your family. Create a safe space for everyone to express their thoughts and feelings. As previously mentioned, it always shows unconditional love. Demonstrate your love and support for your bonus children, regardless of their behavior or circumstances. Let them know your love is unconditional; they could do nothing to make you love them less.

While pouring all this love into your bonus children, do not forget to nurture your own well-being. Stepparenting can be demanding, so it's essential to prioritize your own well-being. Practice self-care regularly. Engage in activities that nourish your mind, body, and spirit. Make time for hobbies, exercise, and relaxation.

As mentioned in previous chapters, seek support. Don't hesitate to seek support from your partner, friends, family, or a therapist. Being a bonus parent is challenging, and it's important to have a support system.

Celebrate your achievements as a stepparent, recognizing that you are making a difference in the lives of your bonus children. You don't have to ace it from the start; you are all learning your place in the new family dynamic. Embrace the unique beauty of blended families. Blended families are unique and beautiful in their own way.

Wear your bonus parenthood as a badge of honor. Celebrate the diversity of your family. Appreciate the diversity of your blended family and the unique perspectives each member brings. Embrace the richness of your family's history and experiences. Create your own definition of family. Don't let societal expectations define your family. Create your own definition of family based on love, respect, and connection.

Build a family that works for you. Millennials are a force to be reckoned with, unlike past generations. Most of us either begin or will one day be a bonus parent. We are at a different time from our grandparents and even our parents. Reach out to those like you; find your tribe. Connect with other stepparents and blended families. Sharing experiences and support can be invaluable.

The long-term rewards of being a bonus parent are infinite. The journey of stepparenting, while challenging, is ultimately rewarding. As with your biological children, hopefully, your relationship with your bonus children is lifelong, even if you and your partner part ways or they pass away. If you have the opportunity to build lasting relationships with your bonus children, just do it. These relationships can bring immense joy and fulfillment. You are creating a legacy of love and acceptance for future generations. Your blended family is a testament to the power of love to overcome challenges.

If you were not a parent before becoming a bonus parent, you may experience a need for accelerated personal growth and transformation. Stepparenting can be a catalyst for personal growth and transformation. You will learn valuable lessons about love, patience, and resilience. Enjoy the journey, celebrate the milestones, and cherish the moments of connection. You are building something beautiful and unique.

Let's expand on "Enjoy the Journey," focusing on the subtle nuances of finding joy and fulfillment and cultivating a lasting sense of peace within the often-complex world of stepparenting. Bonus parents must cultivate mindfulness and presence. The journey is best enjoyed when you're fully present in the moment. Practice mindfulness by paying attention to the details of everyday experiences. Savor the small moments. Savor the warmth of a hug, the sound of laughter, or the beauty of a sunset.

You don't have to be a supermom. Give yourself grace. This is an area I have struggled with personally. Let go of perfectionism. Release the pressure to create perfect moments or achieve unrealistic expectations. Embrace the imperfections and find beauty in the messy reality of family life.

Do not neglect your romantic relationship with your partner in a quest to be a super bonus parent. You must disconnect to connect. Put away distractions like phones and devices to fully engage with your stepchildren and partner. Create dedicated time for screen-free interactions.

Remember to nurture your inner child. Rediscovering your own sense of playfulness can bring joy to both you and your bonus children. Embrace spontaneity. Be open to spontaneous adventures and activities. I'm not encouraging you to abandon structure or schedules, but every so often, throw caution to the wind. Let go of rigid schedules and embrace the freedom to play.

Rediscover your hobbies. Engage in activities you enjoyed as a child. This can reignite your sense of wonder and creativity. Play with your bonus children. Join in their games and activities. Play a video game with them, roll around on the floor with them, play hide-and-seek with them, take a walk, have a spa day, go to a game arcade—the list is endless. This shows them you're interested in their world and creates opportunities for bonding.

Finding meaning and purpose in your role as a bonus parent is in your best interest. Stepparenting can be a deeply meaningful and purposeful endeavor. Focus on your values. Reflect on your core values and how they guide your actions as a bonus parent. Live your values authentically and model them for your bonus children. Recognize that you are creating a legacy of love and acceptance for your blended family. Your actions will shape the lives of your bonus children for years to come.

For your own well-being, find purpose in service. Look for opportunities to serve your family and community. Helping others can bring a sense of purpose and fulfillment. While serving others, you are essentially building a supportive community. You don't have to navigate the stepparenting journey alone. Connect with other bonus parents. Join support groups or online communities for stepparents. Sharing experiences and advice can be invaluable.

As with your romantic relationship, don't neglect your social ones either. Stay connected with your social circle and nurture your friendships. Maintain strong friendships and social connections. These relationships provide emotional support and a sense of belonging. Older family members can provide tools and strategies for navigating the challenges of stepparenting that you may not have considered.

Cultivate inner peace. Finding inner peace is essential for enjoying the bonus parenting journey. Be sure to practice self-compassion. Be kind and compassionate to yourself, especially during challenging times. Acknowledge your imperfections and learn from your mistakes.

Let go of resentment. Forgive yourself and others for past hurts. In a perfect world, all members of blended families would get along. This is not usually the case, so challenge yourself to always rise above pettiness. Resentment only weighs you down and prevents you from moving forward. Find moments of solitude. Schedule time for solitude and reflection. This can help you recharge and gain clarity. Embrace the impermanence of life. Recognize that life is constantly changing. Embrace the impermanence of moments and cherish the present. There is a priceless gift in growing as a bonus parent. Stepparenting is a journey of continuous growth and transformation. Embrace the learning process. View challenges as opportunities for learning and growth. Be open to new perspectives and approaches.

Celebrate your strengths. I am a very organized person and great at hosting events. My mother always made our birthdays memorable. I loved how special it made me feel. I love seeing the smiles on my kids' faces on their birthdays when they feel special and celebrated. Acknowledge and celebrate your strengths as a stepparent. Just by being present, you are already positively impacting the lives of your bonus children.

Find joy in the process of bonus parenthood. Remember that the journey itself is the reward. Find joy in the process of building relationships and creating a loving family. By cultivating mindfulness, finding meaning, and nurturing your inner peace, you can truly enjoy the stepparenting journey and create a fulfilling and joyful life for yourself and your blended family.

Let's explore the profound and often overlooked aspects of "Enjoying the Journey," especially in the context of long-term stepparenting and the evolving dynamics of blended families. Finding peace amidst ambiguity. Blended families often navigate a landscape of ambiguity, where roles and relationships are fluid and evolving. Embracing the "Gray Areas." Learn to tolerate ambiguity and accept that there may not always be clear-cut answers or solutions. Flexibility and adaptability are your allies.

When navigating the unpredictable aspects of bonus parenthood, understand that life in a blended family can be unpredictable. Cultivate a sense of inner peace by accepting that you cannot control everything and finding stability within yourself. Focus on building inner stability and resilience rather than seeking external validation or control. Your inner peace becomes a source of strength for the whole family.

Master the art of letting go of expectations. Unrealistic expectations are a common source of disappointment and frustration in stepparenting. Letting go of the "perfect family" myth will save you much heartache. Let go of the idealized notion of a "perfect family." Embrace the unique and imperfect beauty of your blended family.

Do your best to detach from outcomes. Focus on the process of building relationships, rather than fixating on specific outcomes. Trust that your efforts will bear fruit in time. Accept that you and your bonus children are on different timelines. Recognize that everyone in the blended family will adjust at their own pace. Avoid comparing your family's journey to others.

Cultivate a sense of wonder and discovery. Stepparenting can be an opportunity to rediscover the world through the eyes of a child. Embracing that childlike curiosity. Cultivate a sense of wonder and curiosity about the world. Explore new experiences and learn alongside your bonus children. Discover new perspectives through them. Be open to learning from your bonus children and seeing the world from their unique perspective. This can broaden your horizons and deepen your understanding.

Lean into the power of self-acceptance and self-compassion. Stepparenting is a journey of self-discovery and growth. Embrace your imperfections and recognize that you are doing your best. Self-compassion is essential for navigating the challenges of bonus parenting.

Even the most ordinary moments of daily life can be filled with meaning and joy. Practice mindfulness during everyday tasks, such as cooking, cleaning, or driving. Find beauty and meaning in the present moment. A simple conversation or a shared laugh can strengthen your bond. I appreciate the beauty of imperfection. Find beauty in the imperfections of daily life. Embrace the messiness and unpredictability of family life.

Ultimately, "Enjoying the Journey" is about creating a legacy of love and growth for your blended family. Build a foundation of love and acceptance. Create a foundation of love, acceptance, and respect that will support your family for years to come. Inspire growth and resilience in your children. Inspire all your children to grow and develop into resilient and compassionate individuals. Leave a positive impact on your children. Recognize that your actions as a bonus parent are positively impacting all your children's lives. Your biological children will remember how you treated their siblings, and hopefully, they will model your behavior if they ever have the honor of being a bonus parent themselves.

By cultivating inner peace, embracing imperfection, and finding meaning in the mundane, you can truly enjoy the stepparenting journey and create a fulfilling and joyful life for yourself and your blended family.

Chapter 8: Summing it up

The process of reflecting and moving forward. We've journeyed through the intricacies of stepparenting, exploring the challenges, the joys, and the ever-evolving dynamics of blended families. Now, let's take a moment to reflect on the key takeaways and chart a course for continued growth and harmony. Being a bonus parent is like weaving a tapestry.

As with a tapestry, each strand intertwines with the others and affects the overall look of your garment. Likewise, every interaction, occasion, and exchange between you and your bonus children affects how the overall journey will be.

To recap, let's go over the items shared in the book:

Respecting Boundaries: We emphasized the importance of respecting the biological parent's role and understanding one's place within the family structure. This isn't about diminishing one's role but rather clarifying it for everyone's well-being.

Building Bridges, Not Walls: Communication, empathy, and patience are the cornerstones of building strong relationships with your bonus children. We explored how to create a welcoming environment and foster trust.

Navigating Conflict and Discipline: We delved into the complexities of discipline, highlighting the importance of consistency, communication, and understanding of your role as a supportive adult.

Blending Families During Special Occasions: We discussed strategies for navigating holidays, birthdays,

and other significant events, emphasizing flexibility, compromise, and the creation of new traditions.

The Power of Self-Reflection

We stressed the importance of "checking yourself," recognizing your triggers and biases, and practicing emotional regulation.

Enjoying the Journey

We encouraged you to find joy in the everyday moments, cultivate mindfulness, and embrace the unique beauty of your blended family.

Now, let's explore the key principles for ongoing success. As you move forward on your stepparenting journey, remember these essential principles: Patience is paramount. Building strong relationships takes time. Be patient with yourself, your partner, and your bonus children.

Communication is crucial. Open, honest, and respectful communication is essential for navigating the complexities of blended family life. Empathy is essential. Try to see things from your bonus children's perspective and empathize with their feelings.

Consistency provides stability. Consistent routines, rules, and expectations can create a sense of stability and security for children. Flexibility is key. Blended family life is rarely predictable. Be prepared to adapt to changing circumstances and adjust your approach as needed.

Self-care matters. Don't neglect your own needs. Prioritize self-care to maintain your emotional well-being. Seek support when needed. Don't hesitate to seek support from your partner, friends, family, or a therapist.

Looking ahead to continued growth and adaptation. Stepparenting is a dynamic and evolving process. Embrace lifelong learning. Stay open to learning and growing as a parent overall. Seek out resources, attend workshops, and engage in ongoing self-reflection.

You must adapt to changing needs. As your bonus children grow and develop, their needs will change. Be prepared to adapt your approach to stepparenting accordingly. Remember to celebrate the milestones and transitions in your stepchildren's lives. These celebrations can strengthen family bonds and create lasting memories.

Create a love, acceptance, and respect culture within your blended family. Remember that every family is unique. What works for one family may not work for another. Do not be afraid to find the system that works best for your specific family.

There are a multitude of rewards of bonus parenting. A major one is the legacy of love you will leave. Your bonus children will remember the love and affection you showed them for the rest of their lives. The era of the "evil stepmother" stereotype is over! Kill any notion of it within you. You are contributing to the creation of a loving and supportive family environment.

You have the privilege of witnessing your bonus children's growth and transformation. You are leaving a legacy of love and acceptance that will be passed down to future generations.

In conclusion, as you continue your bonus parent journey, remember you are not alone. Embrace the challenges, celebrate the joys, and cherish the moments of connection. You are making a difference in the lives of your bonus children, and your love and support will have a lasting impact.

Signed,

Levi's Bonus Parent :)